Unrestricted Moment: The chance of real discovery [sic]... best achieved *in the process* of writing; being open to the surprise *within oneself* – that difficult place where 'world' and 'language' interact, determining outcomes (±). Against which demand for tribute, the individual knowingly or unknowingly plots a course.

The book's first section deals with the vagaries of the creation process as the artist encounters them; the second acknowledges the nagging stimulus of nature; and the third navigates 'the ordinary', its urgencies and ennui. Overlapping all is a detailed realisation of the slipperiness of *perception* and how chancy the words that conjure it.

Peter Dent was born in Forest Gate, London in 1938. He married and began taking writing seriously in the early Sixties. After working in offices and a library he trained for teaching, which he retired from in 1991. He ran Interim Press for twelve years, publishing a number of books by or on individual writers and artists; his own work has appeared in many pamphlets, magazines and anthologies. He currently lives in Budleigh Salterton, Devon, where he continues his 'negotiations with words'.

Unrestricted Moment

Unrestricted Moment

Peter Dent

UNRESTRICTED MOMENT
© 2002 Peter Dent

ISBN 1 900152 76 2

Cover art © Kit Surrey
Cover design by Neil Annat

Acknowledgements
Fire, Shearsman

Published by
Stride Publications
11 Sylvan Road, Exeter
Devon EX4 6EW
England

www.stridebooks.co.uk

Stride Publications
85 Old Nashua Road
Londonderry, NH 03053
USA

www.stridebooks.com

Contents

Adjacent Drumming

Late Reading   *13*
Navigating   *14*
The Hold   *15*
Quotas This Day   *16*
Treated Text   *17*
Reconnections   *18*
Corrections   *19*
Equivalence   *20*
Making of Words   *21*
If Anywhere   *22*
Disputed...   *23*
Meantime Making   *24*
Score   *25*
By Neglect   *26*
Routine Exchanges   *27*
Countermelody   *28*
Extension   *29*
Out Under Heaven   *30*
Late Night Ploy   *31*
Thinking Cloud   *32*
Content   *33*
Connectives   *34*
Velocities   *35*
Impressions   *36*
Displacements   *37*
Intentions   *38*
Epigraphs   *39*
To Legislation   *40*

Natural Order

Autumn/Winter: Sequencing   *43*
Spring Balance   *44*
Access (Alternative)   *45*
Four Investigations (with Birds)   *46*

November Bird with Tree *47*

Winter Arrivals: Resources *48*

Serious Flowers *49*

Avoidance *50*

Song Thrush *51*

Dry Season *52*

Spring Vessel *53*

Tidal Reach: Overnight *54*

Landfall: 'Unto Day' *55*

Firmament *56*

Unconducted Ceremony *57*

Fiction *58*

Ash *59*

Substance *60*

First Thing *61*

Palette *62*

Cancellation *63*

Daylight In *64*

Salt in the Wind *65*

Box Tree Garden with Figure *66*

Business Park *67*

Withheld Particulars *68*

Necessary Burning

From Monochrome *71*

Turning Form *72*

Application *73*

Advent *74*

Brown Field Site *75*

Redirections *76*

'The Card Players' *77*

Circulation *78*

According to Plan *79*

Articulation 1967 (BRB) *80*

Questions of Completion *81*

Resources *82*

Acceptable Currency *83*

One Side of Littoral   *84*
Last Gravity   *85*
South   *86*
For a Mirror   *87*
Material Time   *88*
Reworking Exits   *89*
On Dipped Lights   *90*
Governing Fashion   *91*
Nothing Special   *92*
Press Release   *93*
HM&S Late Night Ferry   *94*
Dispensation   *95*
Speaking Up   *96*
Primary Education   *97*

...you cannot observe a wave without
bearing in mind the complex features
that concur in shaping it and the other,
equally complex ones that the wave
itself originates.

Italo Calvino, *Mr Palomar*

Adjacent Drumming

Late Reading

Hard down this road from the city   night

Of the endless/troubling   the small found words
The misdemeanours of a life   now back from
Its running   back to the point: the rehearsing of

'Home' under lights   being here   are we anywhere?
Love   it can leave us   *unknowing*   as ghosts
With their *ever & ever*   strange lights   so hard

On the wording   the 'who' we occasion and 'story'
Whose nothing is true   is it...   loving
My conscript of forces   etc   and ever

That sees it   this emptying   *night* into form?

Navigating

Lyme Bay nights

Imagine then   this making for a poem
Intervals events white water   churning at
The ship of state   'made ready'   forging

Steel plate wisdom   keeping nothing back
No words except know perfectly the way
Each side the prow they have to fall   now

Venture   nothing gained what else   imagine
Please   long straits awinding   even hours'
Long watch to see a ship of fools pass by

Hove to in plenty   dark   as a nightmare
Echo sounding who we are   our place in
Waves a wave could still   make ground to be

The Hold

The transient makes it in again for refit   Winter

Starlit pages and thinking   ever to co-exist

Where it's hand-to-hand   or mouth   and who
Would bet on it   this city by the river
In its dithering hard perfection   its carried
Over losses   all so clear when my ship comes in
Let's say   to freezing far from ordinary lights
Quick commerce and easy violence   a love to

Write home about   the old hands still at work

Engaging measure   words   in reconstructed time

Quotas This Day
Southwest Approaches

At work   at war with it   delirium

    daring to know its tides
    well *out of the swing of*   just

Rehearsing   look another day   we are

    unconscious of   the thought
    it is we choose   who have

The right to ransack next   a dreaming

    into turquoise   shoals
    quick acids   wrack now

Life's unsayable   *a world we do arrest*

    by all we say   hard drawn
    to it   small sketches only

Dare we net   of silver   in its dearth

Treated Text

Habits   of learning 'a re-imagined landscape'

Looking to know one's mind   to move   as if
One had any say in it   whatever it is   this
Slow turning of a tendril through a day   green

Thought   and whether the thing's locked in
Or under starlight under cover   of a mind
To leak away   seeing what value in the end's

Subsumed   made re-available in like to one
Who asks who stumbles on it   so travels on
And through   amazed   how once I thought it

Mattered   all of it really   somewhere rhymes

Reconnections
like keeping spanners in the works

'Sensing' time   and again there'll be the word
It goes with   'atmosphere'   collapsing
As someone then another leaves the room

Not how to put a stop to things   but
More to know   come outside in   just one
As love might   some time   all it is

Soft light   played out across a moment
Making it clear   in part   it underlines
The title   even the cover photograph

I have for just this small investigation
Random sources I'm loathe to put at risk
Now out   preparing meaning   as they must

For a certain look on a certain face
Today's not giving in to   endless rewrites
Wants no shadows   *somewhere somehow*

Is a world   revealed?   the question's out
And order brokering no deal just teases
Brings this preface staring to...   [a close?]

Corrections

Misfiring   and cold as a morning gets
I work at all the loose connections   letters
That failed to say   *speak now or*   said

Too much   won't let my mystery in
With more   it's 'ice' now glinting on a wing
What else   from here to there   unsettled

Distances   connecting bright and ordinary
Planes   a trail of particles   Godsend
The words   if only   here no measure

Lets me plan for restoration   grief
What chance procedures am I into   dark
Where someone else's proof sets up

Hard type   and harder editing lets those
Who read pick up the clues   forgive
My winter metaphors   a 'world' stands by

Equivalence

Daybook fantasy   to pressure meaning
Of my own whose colours live to vary
Simply into that which is   all right

Itself   before I bring myself to bear
Replete   no never never   worlds
can't have too many ways to read

A day when skies are dangerous   if
Clear   there's work to do   inscriptions
To be loaded up   as maybe   truth is

Here   long suffering all my words
When easterlies bite hard a harder going
Still   yet give my weighing up a lift…

Cold hands know nothing of this   but
Better know themselves   how life proves
Heady   weightless as the stuff of words?

Making of Words

Another day   and the vowels
Soon words of a *huge wind* leave
Both me and guesswork open

The sky is a riot of greys
Collision and chaos free as
Maybe it wouldn't seem   as

Nothing else is   holy   only in
Completion   signed and sealed
Wrapped round a dream

Makes 'nothing'   tangible
Reality   I wonder   all it wants
If there and truly through it

Makes some sense   *another day*
I'll key e.g. these fair few in   watch
How   *watch how they blow*?

If Anywhere

Inexact?   the world I travelled
Out to see   on schedule   but within
Breaks words   look   how it rains

Comes shadow   out of every stanza
Substance   and who will listen there
In real resourceful time   this brief

A daydream complementing fact
Its healthy noise   adjacent drumming
Till the message clears   well

Need we nothing more than need?
Bizarre design   and fearful storm
Shall I at loggerheads with *whom*

My old familiar call it 'light' that
Makes the first true break and traffics
Free of words   amazed   we'll see

Disputed...
a sonnet for meaning

And then the word for 'temperature'
Is not the half of it   which word is
Melting   pertinent to 'iron'?   but
Don't stay up for it   the mind leaps
Neatly over bridges maybe metaphors
It quite if not exactly since mid-air's
No place to be   makes argument out
Of no-goes by degree and anywhere

Is nowhere we can know   forget it
If this much else shows up   its white
On screen its fizzing horizontals oh
Do speak us nice expletives   never
Hear'd the like of half-thoughts hardly
Up to it Plan B to goto   cancel mind

Meantime Making

1

Obituary the clouds
From which the crow flies
Awkward over lilies
And paragraphs where light
Has trouble breaking in

2

Graphic skies with twilight
Evidence we've seen
The best of it hardpressed
The word along the shore
Is darkness soon so long

3

Life overwinters thought
There's nothing now but this
Familiar light down nerves
That makes a window anxious
For your silhouette

Score

Convoluted   and you said it
Life prepares   the notes and

Plays I hear 'prepared piano'
Knowing a trick or two dispenses

But the half of it   unknown
To love it when it comes to this

Dark children off the leash out
Dancing   all my lyric's maze

By Neglect

You say you're not looking for any
Particular way to go...   at least

You have no notion there is or may
Yet be somehow some way to go

And you are arriving at a word
And selecting another to follow so

Everyday you barely know it
No contra-indications and maybe

Not unknown to art the small
And patient possibility acted out

Of love establishing the ground
It feels should feel you're safe on

Knowing there's nothing left and
Much much more you'd care to say

Routine Exchanges

on re-hearing John Coltrane's 'Naima'

Your song into birdless grey wet air
Dissolves   its now dead voice   sound

If you put me to it's 'tawny'   timely
I'd been thinking lately of its
Cutting and thoughtful edge   as yet

Another grey   well may it   sound be
'Stone'...   are not we now   in con–
Versation   sharing terms like these

But redistributing something of our
Selves?   oh dear an other world   no
Make that plural   where the word is

Out   through soft distinctive air
Which you   who hear it are   you now

Countermelody
where night meets day

Objects of his dream   here's decadence

To take this *present* out of bounds to
Have the thing revisioned and revised
Made perfect calm and steady   moonlight

Through his window   dreams forever
At the ready and amazed   through which
World showing shadow any need

He felt the need they urged to press

Extension

for Lee Harwood

A morning in August   early
The book says   trembling   a hint
Of mist here   a softness   taking
The colours out of words

The *fondness* of the last *farewell*
To dwell on   knowing again there's
Nothing here but low-key small
Digression making its point

For comfort much too close
To home   listening through the many
Sounds to the sound of a ladder
Raised   its aluminium   light

And tough   to follow carry out
Instructions   my reckoning
Everything in words   a deal too airy
Light   soft colours for a world

The painters know   and tremble
Devious and *fugitive*   if not
The former   so experience dictates
Will *not be seen before your eyes*

Out Under Heaven

Handmaid   and barely a star

Which presence cancelled in
A street of footsteps finding
Cold within   which part of
Speech will then excite itself
To come and file new entries

Ravishing   a text about to be
Discovered thinking   lights
Here shining down to fumble
For engage   as who believes
An other world not out of

Step at all   can softly breathe

Late Night Ploy

Discerning nothing   thought considers it
Habitually   as good a way as any
To break the sequence   days on end

And getting nowhere   take the high wire
And the canyon   put a name to it
This game of chance will soon be over

Sounds of water   not difficult to make
The other easy thing   the falling
Clean notation for oneself   look hard

Thinking Cloud

And nothing   to look for here until
The need   as I imagine it a greyness
Still some way from home   from rain

Blue...   painterly and unmysterious?
Who cares how deep   downgrading now
To black as the need floats quietly in

To ride   maybe or not   such surfaces
Immaculate control of   not quite nothing
A strangeness   cancelled in a moment

Or complicating   barely   an hour and
I *might* come to a sense of it   the world
Believing in it   only   as I thought

Content

A 'coloured woodcut'   half of which
Is black   one figure holds a lamp

A light for another   and the shrub
She's holding searching   now for one

Long moment turns her head   a question
Travelling   no telling who is asking

Makes for meditation   plainly
Harunobu's work   he calls it *Capturing*

the Grasshopper   so much green
To lose it in   his question   lies

In wait   and they are more than ready
Here's the little wooden box

Connectives

And put the leaf back   on the tree
So break the rule   no hardship
To the mind   the barest movement

Move the word   from here to there
Not stopping to   as I do here
Debate   each shade of green   let

Gravity be   nothing   Summer
Long   but just a word   connecting
Light   to what we need   to fix

Velocities

Measuring   as if one has to   dust
The last event   its filigree of all
That came before   abbreviated   barely

Visible components   tooled with colour
And time   now   as the crow flies
Merely such and such   watched then

Or not   unwondered with a will
All questions later   down to matters
Of escape   grey sky   the size of it

Impressions

There's so much to be said   a forest
Exhaustive   ever on its way   to evening
Where desire makes good   lost light

And lexicons   a single shadow aching
At a desk   for whom the word
Must play   no stranger   to redress

The book is slow   about its leaves
Turns over states   ideas   to warm us
With regret   new truth   outlasting lives

Displacements

What's ordinary   out of words tonight
Is oceanic   overriding   with forces
Heady and huge   at work   at large in it

The atom even   where we move   and
Scarcely know we move   I have you
In my heart   a whole world   providential

Under sail   and love   more than we guess
Is steady   conscious   in disclaiming
Self   for all the wealth   and play of it

Intentions

Being   the very bridge   it's here
I am   maintaining common ground
As mind   dear one   in making it

Is elevated   into strangeness
Light   who is it moves   I come to
Such accomplishment   to words

A lift to structure   whole   as can be
Made   this loving   steely framework
Holding   gale force what   in place

Epigraphs

White stone   a colonnade   and distance
In a conversation   words reworked
From almost nothing   but the past

Looks on   aggrieved   can't find its name
In this name   shifting sands   a gleam
As words go down   again   with sunset

Trying every text   hard questions
Levelled at the dark   who shaped
The stone   barefaced   is making clear

To Legislation

re. letting it all in

So looking to see it   *Wood*   the picture
There   come back   long shadows falling
To the eye   peel everything we makar
Cannot make away   still more   remember

Pulling over hard   the slow lane slowing
Intervals where wicked constructs stepped
Their stately dance   who found no void
Of choice   then check the flow   approve

At crossroads all the play   meticulous
With properties that gravitate to words
To tremble   newness   like an eye whose
Wanderlust's insatiable   as birches grasses

Meaning malachites are driven through
Event and beyond   check impulse: *eventide*
Said someone   who the shadow is   will I
Be shadow again   I can't stay here forever

Surface blind   remaining what miraculous
Undeviating?   maybe misappropriating
Light   is this what this is   angels falling
Out of context   where the weather holds?

Natural Order

Autumn / Winter: Sequencing

Discrete and undervalued tones   in anything
From mud to rust   now little yellows look
Are desperate to entertain   a truce as some
Describe it   and whether or not to hear it

Shall we wonder   how new cold preoccupies
The skin   the quickest of words   *alert to*
Aren't we just at last these *facts*   exceptional
Exceptional if seasonal   in hope on hope

Too far   to sketch the long free-wheeling
Leaves   November   knowing the thin red line
Can't name it   never clearly   sense it maybe
Even here   in its simple structure   braving

Ice   that breathing out and into trust   as
If the moment's not discovered it   already
Almost numberless   wherever one by one
A life is   walked through love's new white

Spring Balance

the wasting of hawthorn hazel & co

Admitted   a visitation of words
Of occasion to the sense of 'glade'
(Who thinks no plan is better

Than the next: to be removed
Who operates bizarre adjustable
Green accounts that no-one till

Tomorrow sees and bleeds by:
Ditto)   *things it is*   *and not*
Appearances to live   distinction

Needed?   here is 'light' you could
Say's quite another thing oh *and*
Appearance having the nerve to deal

In truth   susbtantiating this al-
Beit late amendment   'wren song'
Sung tremendum   quite uncosted

Non-provisional   which here keys in
A future   words as 'dappled' 'sun-
Light'   live and breaking through

Access (Alternative)

To frost   too many leaves and hues
Accompany the annual check
For evidence   of passage   small ones

Scurrying   leaving colours warm
And tangible   in print   ideas
Soon terrified   and plain as time

Comes hard   down words to nothing
Here   this deal of traffic's willed
(And more than time) to be itself

For once   *What thought would think*
About might make 'reality'
But not the truth   no 'uniform'

And no excuse to bring us here
Just this   respect   faint withering
Of worlds rephrased   poor glimmer

Abstract as a year   and name   as
Who goes here and watches   words
To leave behind   turn down a page

Four Investigations (With Birds)

Disquisition   late   a dipper to water
Breaking paragraphs   a hundred forms where
Light makes complex   *there*   are nothings
Falling?   a strictness for tomorrow   deep
And crimson   gifted towers of glass to tell

Deregulation   promises   free as blackbirds
In an undergrowth of song   sing who goes there
Connect by rights reserved the what to whom
Offloading 'incident'   here look a cache
Of apples   commerce   can't you tell the din

Dictation   not exactly   as it was
Two buzzards whirl across parentheses
Familiar light   anxiety   the word to keep
In touch with   happenings to prey   why
Not believe or hope   no fall will break

Denouement   demoiselles with parasols
Having their way through aqua   mud   the dead
In raptures   coloured rags the jackdaws eye
Revetments   flags' convenience to cover
Darkness   not the least uncrafted praise

November Bird with Tree

'Awash'   some might describe it
Trunk blown stiffly landward   where
I set it down   in variations

Every year come three decades
The *new* that's maybe   goldfinch

Dazzle   as much in any hands
Worth more...   from ice-cold drizzle
Not yet seen to fall   in flight

From stanzas clipped to nothing   after
All   the place that's recommended's

New and bare   one blackthorn   pouring
Out to face another   flying
And would-be well-groomed year

Winter Arrivals: Resources
wigeon, Brent geese, avocet
  (Otter Valley)

The watching over   and the eye
Returns it   there is this
A glitter on the water   or is it

A glitter there *and* water   lexicon
And variation   keeping open
Trusting in the world we make

Of things   together and apart
Both two and two and four   so
As to have them work   this kind

Of work   their fullness in us
Understanding   meeting the dark cloud
Out of which they fall   alight

Serious Flowers

Keyed in   fair moral eloquence
And all that comes of pain   where we
Are at the end of it   his question

Steeped in oh connecting *things*
Immortal   should it well work out
Be so   be certain what it's not

The 'I' come through   that much
(Etc)   but right to dwell on   good for
Pitching camp on   stanzas   early

Out as always   having the *Morning*
Glory make it   blue and somewhat
Fearful   dark eyes down oblivious

To the bee   who's raiding heavenly
Candour would be so discreet...
Confused in worldly consolation

Avoidance

Black   towering in late-night trees and
Columns   words to nominate and run
Down nothing   not a mist in sight could
Be much worse imagined on the page

Than here   a lifetime bringing to bear
Its woods and white   okays the theme
Continuously   rewinding realism   and
Soon in next-to-nothing's worked up

Order there's a leaf to take from dream
Remember Autumn shall I   catching fire
Sees every shadow out   dispels what
Cannot choose this moment   come to be

Song Thrush

The existence of   the semblance of
Another midnight past   which tier
Of the mind will hold it when the thing
In question's skewed   past midnight

Sounds this singing   one to one
I'd say enough for history   another
Chapter loaded   as I drift to sleep
An hour another hour   hypnotic

Foregrounds   out of which a wing
Will travel   veer   can't guess
Which way it goes or what the song
Returns me to   I hear the mind

Dry Season

Old debts old scores   possession is
Barely a stream   not worth a name

But shows on every little map it
Knows what it's up against wants none
Of it   hard writing off   a jolting
Out of what seemed true design

As driven through the world   stark
Colour   flow   and instant deviation
Becomes – it cannot deal with this
High Summer   dereliction into duty

Come what may – what any stream
Becomes when days dry up   the place
Itself   no need to make the point
No case at all to answer   finds

Some levelling in any eye that sees
The lie   instructive   of the land

Spring Vessel

Sun through blinds
And I'm remembering

It wasn't yesterday but
Here on lines of water
All at risk as well

We knew the city
Words we are familiar
With the flood just

Floated out beneath
An April sky Venetian
Blue I watch them note

Their cool renewed
Horizons of ourselves

Tidal Reach: Overnight

Sailing of which

And whatever metaphor
You care mysteriously
About   long out
Unstoppably on theory's

Unconsoling script   sets
Fall in words   unglossed
As anyway they'd know it
We are gravitational and

Human   mind our small
Divine machinery for
Places   oh the waves mark
Smoothly out   we visit

If we dare   by dark
To know 'the knowable'...
Such blades we pull on
Dripping signatures of life

Speaking of which

Landfall: 'Unto Day'

Days after   working out this stretch
Of common water   lines connecting us
The smudge of dark we are   now

Fast on someone's bright horizon
Worse with what's below   nets down
Forever made and mended   true to

Life   gerundive   we are every hope
Slow turning on a day's blue hinge
Cold hands again   who know us

Know it's quite enough to deal with
Hard perception   and nothing here
Will make it easy   to our hold

Small lives at work   strung out of
Hours' pale filament   come bless
This homemade flickering   each lamp

Firmament

January   moves into the shadow
Of nothing   more complex   but
A different way of thinking

The thing through   early   fast
Falling snows   always to be (in
Memory)   enough to act it out

Not doubt appearances   mind
Taking the next line on   is whose?
Congenial to the question mark

That's mine to weave   material
Destiny   if so so run   read
Nothing into it   things settle

As they will   as deep as maybe
Truth   banked up I am   so
Cold against established signs

Unconducted Ceremony

Malt Hill, Egham

Places   where the paths cross   histories
Of a single Winter   snowfall   never
To let me take you out of context

Children silent on a sledge   dropping
Down away   past orchards ornament   to
Where one senses the beginnings almost

Of an equilibrium   uncomposed   whose
Sentences race clear to never-never   haunted
By a look   a light   no single truth

Fiction

Happening   in words   your landscape's

Turning   knowing   how I move

With ease from place to place   unarmed

And longing   looking out   for you

Through unglazed windows   happy as

The ghosts made out of it   this calling

(Endless means)   come true   my sounds

Stack up   and...   *tallest darkest tors*

As read *fall silent   even unto*   scree

Ash

So maybe   maybe not   a restlessness

In branches   or even who at last

It is will be here…   colours

Gathered to the mind   exaggerating

With this litany of   *(thinking)*

Minor windforms   simply too much

Resting on it   all   too much a flutter

A bet there never was   and will be

Only when we get to it   true song

Substance

In the gleam of that day...   what

Did I make of it   all that revising

Maybe improvising on   (not clear)

The simplest version   detail there

Of   *goldfinches hurtling over gorse*

No   not quite as it was   but ever my

Attention / intention   still   to take

The breath   late Summer's easy

easier now   away   *to see them fly*

First Thing

Weed-woven

The river of shadows
Shingle-broken

Childhood   where I
Wouldn't be   without

These sequences as long
As words are   healing

Held to   and driven
Over line-breaks to

Begin   again the boat
Moves off   as difficult

As knowing...   slow
Across the real of water

Time-stilled lilies
Stitching time

Rain-riven

Palette

after Agnes Martin

Breaking meditation   the petals of a rose

On darkness say   but you're not saying
Anything   of colours gathered to a word

You wouldn't carry home   in armfuls
Love   you know it's yours   ...*aum*

Nightlong   the flowers you have in mind

Cancellation

Will we not entirely know it

To unlovely ends but hope for
More   which prime account
Is opened often   a voice

And just an ordinary mist
Through trees will disappear
Long waiting for it   slowly

At first   the wind   is not
Is she not   indescribable the
Nothings of every   look

Here's love   lean into it

Daylight In

kingfisher on a branch, clear water...

...just one scene from many   and in
Whose real occasion intervals are closed
Well this may happen any time   it is

Revealed   but not without a certain
Gift of concentration   owned   but still
An intervention   certainly   the question

There which words italicise and what to do
About the rest   the answer's somewhere
Else and proper knowing   was it something

I said   is overhanging   as in gardens
Planning all those ancient moves   still blue
The world awaits   the flash of a fin

Salt in the Wind

At the edge   at the drop by thorn

Of thinking   the night thinking
Through whatever the seeming or

Not of it   *pictures* me the moments
I *am* to   immediate as would be

Not unrealisable wildness   in
Joy   its shifting intensity   dark

Now   the waters below me are
Spoken   and *louelich of speche*

To be present   and falling enough

Box Tree Garden with Figure

for Ian Robinson

It's managed so well   impermanent abstraction
There's nothing final   but the mind stands by
To move   as satisfying in its singular way as
Any song or dance   set up to close a deal

Makes close-clipped sense of green and darker
Large irregular cones   round which a figure
Peers and calls   in simple revelation   sure
Enough it's not my first time here   late

Always to the spot   an afternoon   September
Maybe with the gates about to close   long
Aren't they often long in poems   shadows
Turning   as I turn look hard at him

The artist   child with more than usual gifts
Expensive no but costly in concern   who has me
Read this day again   find strangeness working
Hard to order   shape as well my last last line

Business Park

the natural order

Refurbished   night-long rain and cold
Translate to systems   unaccounted

For   the way they do things   simply
Sleight of hand   in places   children

Will have come   not easily to know
But we will try   themselves   to witness

Bloody purchase   timed abstractions
Of the real dark   now fired-up with

Billboards seeing the woods the words
Give way   small streams we know we

Might have dammed   those just a start
To quartz and method   off the record

Red with violation   things a memory's
Committed to   leaves crystal   bright

And timed to go   in structures true
To form   informing well-said disrepair

Withheld Particulars

1   Medieval almost   blue in one corner of the sky
strikes out   another hour   disquiet imagines it is
all there is   a choir sings deep and even into stone
the very words I ask

2   Cold at the turning where a blackbird shouts
alarm   through brambles notebooks   changing and
exchanging words   one hears of small considerations
letting the poem be

3   Preoccupation this   a seasonal distrust of colours
listed in the catalogue   so trying to harvest   nothing
but the matter of attention   plain infinitives as written
hang more true

4   Black gradient it isn't   indeterminate   this Winter
keeps its house in order   a perfect to-and-fro set up
of would-be letters   servicing the need that rising
knows its mind

Necessary Burning

From Monochrome

Incomprehensible number   lives and daisies
In the dark field of a lifetime   where
He witnesses *event*   and it's the same event

He must replay   a white remarkable dead sky
Like paper   in the small unwritten hours *where*
Moves the child   no matter his mind grows

Dark with thinking   worlds   and categories
Where things go   who cannot bear to end
The counting   weighing up of chances   all

So brilliant in their distribution   daystars
He will pick   somehow convert   for use
In miracles of colour   a haul of *truth*   come

Good and not too late   the unextinguished
Unextinguishable beauty   *who will be there*
Wrapped in the dark   the lucid light obscure

Turning Form
for the smallest hand

It's time to seek it out   present it wrapped in
Nothing   so here's the child   the brightness

Of a point of rest   mind trying the one thing
Roundness   for every (something) world it's

Up against   and hard   hard learning knows
Delight   the question's absolute   of things so

Many so clearly wrapped   in choice   first
This then that the facets   who can shut them

Shut me down he ponders   knowing lights
At every single turn   whole meanings change

Application

Flare   into all you tell me   dreaming

A sodium light for words   returns
Uncertain   figures   to the place of

No recall   so gradually it stills
At which point   dying   make a break

With declaration   one last time
Is there for us   there can't be further

Clarity   *dreams fade as I*   as much
As nothing stills   your life will have it

So   to argument hard revelation

Advent

There it is   it's happened   once
What can't be now   unhappened

Smoke across the valley   voices
A wave on shingle   suchlike

Given   all things to a world which
Moves to move   some reason

Way back serious   in a life lived
True to time   as dreamed we might

Again   those dreams   still smoking
Guns   and men   long waves

Delighting annals and holy lettered
Stones   dishonestly   I'd say

I know it only too well   daylight's
Carol   happening to sing

Bown Field Site

for Rupert Loydell

As if the 'thought' in this heat's derelict
Dividing light   but where it can't be seen
A secret shadow's anxious to begin

Its argument   life heading out   of learning
With a child who digs   and wields no shovel
No maths that counts   makes nothing   ever

The same dust lifting over rubble   lifts
Investment   golden   through a life that clouds
As someone knows   already calculates it

Where to take the gain and lets the land
Do nothing but accumulate…   unkowingly
Another colour   is this the commentary

I need   between the two split tyres and
Frayed asbestos?   what a smile can do
With green   new fern   its cool reserve

Redirections

1

To be present on horizons   several
beyond *order*   witness   if indeed
we may   to the scale of separation

2

Canzon   doorstep note-cum-summons
to the weight in all things   ways to
occupy ourselves   the last *known world*

3

Laws written in   'perfected' may not
be the word   some combination of
and ditto   devious   to lend *occasion*

4

Crossword clue   upmarket gamble
if you want perception   broke
don't mend it   starmaps' *never was*

'The Card Players'

Underlit   domestic as it may be any
And particular   oh a turn of a card
Wind shaking free the wood   its room

Outside the possibilities   of jack and
Knave with whom I walk   in deference
Out through the weather   footsteps

Easy a rhythm as ever there was   in
Dislocation   dark leaf-litter the roiling
Dream   in which I move and seldom

Is it truth is cornered but collapses
Into nothing… as it plays my hand
This happening or two   like any other

Circulation

1

If this is   and the light *is* vivid
It's time to re-examine everything
Not least the red alarm that sounds
Hours later than the cause   whose
Leaps to clarity are over   done

2

Shops laden   here's the winning
Smile and all you know is yours
First base   and all prediction eking
Out a word's largesse   *o people*
Coming good's the way it goes

3

Anticipation   one can point to it
In several clear directions   degrees
Of urgency   to work with aphorism
Letting her last words through   as
Staples pierce the text   and hold

4

Edging out   from xerox darkness to
Generate a dream of sense   weird
Moments   anything you like can be
Composed   look margins hold and
Hold again   eyes flashing at a touch

According to Plan
with Christmas coming

November enclosure   frost and no mean
Privacy in words   a window for you
You can put your face to   zero in

In a thin light raking town   it's anguish
Servicing the shops with ease   with
Truth and tinsel   fancy goods   well-bred

As if they know it   necessary   laden
I am heavier so   and rusty with the art
Of time   with fiction harrowing my plot

All basics near as dammit guaranteed and
Guilty   should you put your mind to it
Hard singing   to the end of expectation

Knowing   the will to be here slides
Off-limits   nothing exceptional I'm sure
Of life looked into   quite transparent

Questions   'skimming the green estate'
See what you make with them
Undecorated but with luck well-dressed

Articulation 1967 (BRB)

in closure and disclosure

Is it   wisdom central   out of which
This small 'concern' comes   thinking
Gravely   and navigating hard...
In exercise of powers under section 56
   (*The Transport Act of 1962*)

A land that dips and gathers to itself
Spring floods   by the run-down line to
Nowhere   'Dead Man's Burrows'   where
The plough sliced gleaming into bone

It's blues again   so tell me   nothing's
Easy is it   holding on and to the last
Few unsold names who've come and gone
Seen other moves   in train   gross

Product   of our times our interest   so
Slow to drain away   these waters   small
Indiscretions   words we're taught as
Might be really lived   a last train back

All lights and flags still waving   certain
To be caught by true enthusiasts
Come this way   by storm   by time
What else turned up   unmanufactured in
Its element   here chronicled for good

Questions of Completion

1

There's no beyond he said   beyond
Believing it   to be   he sees it
This side   and he doesn't   skipping
Blue   incomprehension   of the eye

2

The basic need   as snowflakes fall
At last   concerns itself with gravity
To catch no single shadow   think
A world is starting out   then go

3

Shock puts a gloss on things   a flight
Of intricate unwanted signs   as well
It may   read here   excite or maybe
You will not   the riot act   for real

4

Grey-white   to underline his story
Taking it nowhere over waves   who
Read the light hard into it...   ghost
A wing   the fact that comes to rest

Resources

this making this rapt attention

Who   hasn't seen it its *plenty*   to engage with
Its many faces   planet   does it say so too

Whose meaning starts to crack   to dematerialise
What novelties we are and make for no good reason

Than to have   daft coloured dreams ill-dreamed
And why   to bless the 'work'   maintain oh

Impossible numbers   gilding the very few who
Call the tune   stupendous error not knowing

The hour the minus whatever it is   let's set
Our watch   and counting   everything must go

Acceptable Currency

1   Into both outside pockets   and why not   the
too real blues and greens of an otherwise empty
day   suffice to say exchanges now are bound to
magnify   with trust here bidding up his world its
canvas   oh and seeming   seems as large as life

2   Accepting it   he has to   sunflowers in their
dialect just can't wait to get away   integrity and
minor variation both make good his world   the
hours dissolve   and into silence unrestricted colour
paints its loss

3   Minute investigations prove to him how signals
— disregard the style — can govern nothing but
themselves   the present's surely lost   who knows
he said to provenance?   and future seeing the
world *was meant* devised another

4   Converted   from unlikely distances   no not
starlight but another scheme of words   it's this or
nothing makes the perfect QED   here entertains
the lavish risks of *now*   unique attachments
where any dark refrain may overload the real

One Side of Littoral
for the notebook

The world moves off again   blue signs

Of reverence   through days half-looked at
Anyone could say   well   didn't they
Deserve more time?   regret came midday

Was it a Tuesday   some dreamy month
Light running out   beyond the point
Beyond the code this deviant works in

Saw it   leaping intervals   you don't say
Leave   as if I'd have the mind to
Any smoke-filled room where friends are

Whirling   whirl it all...   like so

Last Gravity

Only the one vessel leaving
Its contents blue   is this
Surprising   and no hurry

The barometric pressure is
All that it should be   as
Into a future like canvas

Shaking the tenses rework
The invisible   the carried
Faint words of a whisper

For who will observe it
This *moment*   now leaving
Is stretched to the limit

The deal should we say and
We've said it before   of a
Lifetime   anchor to chance

South

Streets of the city   falling   in white

White cubes   wherein a room   to contemplate
A season turbulent with flower   new rhymes
To find you say   though finding put an end

To things lends courage to the words no hour
Can bind   pale limitless enclosures if
You will and I will not disown this place

Where truth and latin love of old exhale

For a Mirror

Oh to be   with simple
Theory   its beautiful
Blue cloud   like day
Clear day   come

Clear of it   complete
Bewilderment   a new
Brush ridding all
Elaboration   shock of

Thing on thing and
Dark   *the tea leaves*
Left   so aren't we
Ever   *in a cup* we're

Brewing   something
Something extraordinary
How purposeful
How plain   we are

Material Time
and the literary myth

Knap or knop   some loop   whatever

In the weave   these places these people
With their fly-blown ancient capitals
And correctly dressed *italics*   slowing

Every time against the eye   unsteady
Eddies in the stream I can't control
Such choice   strange complex taking

The sheen from any run   blue days
How beautiful and clean if I could run
Keep up with them   uninterfered with

Perfect as I want them   ...straight

Reworking Exits

'An abandoned house / full of forgotten talk'
  – Antonin Bartusek

1 Red streaks to the east   intensities can't
wait to come off-shift   again there's no-one
notices who might   her dream is restless
making out lacunae   history   is this the
question   a scrabble in dark abandoned cars

2 Austere   slow air to a narrative   the
morning's lost in its choice of futures   cloud
and the summer house are standing by   as
ever   the dark red flowers of another century
provoke   which words   to weigh her mind

3 It becomes a distance to revere she says
an eloquence of sorts   in peeling plaster   a
hint of smoke through trees as the girl appears
not quite ourselves   that's what we must be
again   unstoppably   the little orchard burns

4 The time and the place for it   her words
intuitive almost   be glad that the spoken word
is done   again to merge with the shadows of
vision   now he can summarise   the night
its mechanisms its brand new range of colours

On Dipped Lights

Thinking the less of it I know   biography's
Unstopping   its scary moment to moment fire
Of information ranging nerves   tomorrows

I'll become   but tiring yawn and stretch
Think safe   where drawn up shady in the text
My *'Deus X'*   immortal limousine

Pulls out   'low overheads low mileage'
So the man said   saw my name go down
For it in duplicate   this once and shiny home

I dream in   'what you wanted yes'   the question
Ran full pelt past maybe nothing   I wouldn't
Have put it quite that way   long views

Escaping   things I might have said   it's
Night remembers most   to counsel words
With criss-cross beams   devout   averting eyes

Governing Fashion
or the election of Spring

The fact of the matter   and more
The constructed *whatever*   (it varies)

That's going on nothing keeps 'words'
Off the streets   we are fit for

A suitable flowering   new money
Ill–lit and as soft as a sub–clause

All that we should be   is weak in
The knees   come good oh a tremens

Mute slinx   *we commend her*   high
On the catwalk   practising grey

Nothing Special

It's about   if you want to know
It   getting mud on your boots

That does it   it's an abstract world
Out there you're into   electronic
Hard-nosed dialectic   high relief

High interest and thresholds under-
Scribed by nothings in the city more
Than futures   more than a single

Change of clothes   try telling them
You're getting a life and a wife
Demutual   it's easier cleaning up

The garage door goes up and over
Touch a button and out she rolls
The gleam   try nature natural like

Getting in touch with the inner man
In Marlboro   not grass but acres
Blue old-fashioned sky   to claim

Your stake   go native   ankle-deep
In abstract's all   is all you need

Press Release
the word was it was out

It was a night to remember   so many and so much
come together   intricate and cosmetic   *Brut* as the
smile I warmed to   the graceful grim good humour
of a text   whose weather laboured later on the 57
smack on time half-lit   I laughed   a good deal
blustery till *Omega* came alive and rolled its all-fresh
green relentlessly up and down the bus   I thought of
nature   closed my eyes like this till no-one moved

HM&S Late Night Ferry

Portico past twilight shadows   up
Against the cream and pastel   doors

About to close   switch off as if
We would   incendiary conditions
For a quiet exchange   instalment

By instalment   quid pro quo
A pleasant wind lifts up her counter
Smile   as nicely does   the words

Laid down   no doubt she keeps
It up this good ship tight   who's
Overboard by night is salivating

Hard   the thought of goods good
Credit in her sea of glass un-tills

Dispensation

1   Unmeaning and only a waterfall   arrived at
power cum threads of light   but it was love
being born   with suspicion encoded   as anyone
writing would know it   a strangeness come
down   and taking the thing apart

2   Grandfather working iron in the dockyard
nights   midwinter mindful of the simplest
structure   to see it go the distance   the
heart of the trade   a necessary burning   and
when it came to it could hardly bear to quit

3   No transcript here   a level too deep for
words   its interested parties meaning-free
it is state I am speaking of   of its magnitudes
grey family interests   loving the bright red
boxes   humbly workably inspired to wreck

4   Containers swung safely over the side   no
crash since when...   but anxiety remembers
the hard re-routing of meanings in the long
strike for home   in the country not years now
speaking   not grievance or tears   but right

Speaking Up

Still meaning a lot   past midnight
Pushing the ferry out   unlit
But time and a half he thought
Was worth it   time to reconvene
Reality   if no-one else would

Speak   negotiate the smallprint
Reef and sandbank   out to get
Things under steam   and nothing
To it   to declare   just interest
In the making capital of lives   so

Putting down a case for flexibility
Blurred edges letting the ship come
Home   well advertised in which
Delight all things contingent shift
To send his mix of once and future

Slanting into newfound waters
Glorious one might say the way
They'd let it through   surreal
Politik   to have their glassy world
Go round dark headlands   grazing

Starlight   early hours' emotion
Carried   to extremes   glossed over
At a price convenient to the party
Meaning never so much come morning
Reconsidered   foundered on a whim

Primary Education

Through which *desert of tortuous attempts*
Was recovered a childhood of the war
Its unspectacular pieces   yellow ochre and
Indian yellow   not privy to other ways:
Look *Mummy* he said the artist the 4–year old
You can't stop time   a pause and   *can you?*
Who'd left a picture in no way incomplete
The man the slant of the head the meaningful
Movement of the arm   one morning shaving
Nothing from the truth in simple lines
La réalité contemplée en solitude n'est pas
Moins la réalité   (of his father)   dreaming
Through a wartime foxed one-shilling Pelican
On art   its line-drawings of primitives
And children ready to ignore the surfaces
Of things   to let their rapid easy lines
Do all the work   investigate and access
Anything whatever   whether here or not
Improbable distances   no less immediate
No special interest in the 'colours' to come
Just self-forgetting lines   a dream that gets
Inside the text   *what is it I'm not*   this life